MARINE
ECOSYSTEMS

by Tammy Gagne

www.12StoryLibrary.com

12-Story Library is an imprint of Bookstaves and Press Room Editions.

Produced for 12-Story Library by Red Line Editorial

Photographs ©: Oleg_P/Shutterstock Images, cover, 1; Jennifer Nicole Buchanan/Shutterstock Images, 4; Frederick J. Horne/Shutterstock Images, 5; Alexander Mazurkevich/Shutterstock Images, 6; Max Earey/Shutterstock Images, 7; Denton Rumsey/Shutterstock Images, 8; Janusz Pienkowski/Shutterstock Images, 9; Zwerver/Shutterstock Images, 10; Maurice Volmeyer/Shutterstock Images, 11; sergemi/Shutterstock Images, 12; Sphinx Wang/Shutterstock Images, 13; Dennis van de Water/Shutterstock Images, 14; BlueOrange Studio/Shutterstock Images, 15; fenkieandreas/Shutterstock Images, 16; Dewald Kirsten/Shutterstock Images, 17, 29 (bottom right); Daniel Poloha/Shutterstock Images, 18; Rich Carey/Shutterstock Images, 19, 29 (top right); bierchen/Shutterstock Images, 20; Conny Skogberg/Shutterstock Images, 21; James Steidl/Shutterstock Images, 22; Kim Briers/Shutterstock Images, 23; Goran Bogicevic/Shutterstock Images, 24; NAN728/Shutterstock Images, 25; Brian S/Shutterstock Images, 26; Leonard Zhukovsky/Shutterstock Images, 27; aquapix/Shutterstock Images, 28 (top); y-studio/iStockphoto, 28 (middle); UnicusX/iStockphoto, 28 (bottom); Natursports/Shutterstock Images, 29 (bottom left)

Content Consultant: Dr. Edward J. Buskey, Professor, Department of Marine Science, The University of Texas at Austin

Library of Congress Cataloging-in-Publication Data
Names: Gagne, Tammy.
Title: Marine ecosystems / by Tammy Gagne.
Description: Mankato, MN : 12 Story Library, [2018] | Series: Earth's
  ecosystems | Audience: Grade 4 to 6. | Includes bibliographical references
  and index.
Identifiers: LCCN 2016047140 (print) | LCCN 2016047927 (ebook) | ISBN
  9781632354587 (hardcover : alk. paper) | ISBN 9781632355249 (pbk. : alk.
  paper) | ISBN 9781621435761 (hosted e-book)
Subjects: LCSH: Marine ecology--Juvenile literature.
Classification: LCC QH541.5.S3 G34 2018 (print) | LCC QH541.5.S3 (ebook) |
  DDC 577.7--dc23
LC record available at https://lccn.loc.gov/2016047140

Printed in China
022017

Access free, up-to-date content on this topic plus a full digital version of this book. Scan the QR code on page 31 or use your school's login at 12StoryLibrary.com.

Table of Contents

Food Is Plentiful in Intertidal Zones

An ecosystem is a group of living things and their physical environment. Many different types of marine ecosystems exist. Each one plays a part in the larger marine ecosystem.

Intertidal zones are located between dry land and the sea.

Sometimes they are underwater. Other times they are above it. When the tide rushes in, these marine ecosystems fill with ocean water. The intertidal zone has a sandy or rocky bottom. It is exposed each time the tide goes back out.

The marine life in intertidal zones must be very hardy. These animals can be pounded by large waves

The Dungeness crab lives along the Pacific coast of the United States.

60 to 90

Percentage of moisture that algae in the intertidal zone lose when the tide goes out.

- Intertidal zones are areas between dry land and the sea.
- Crabs have adapted to the harsh conditions of intertidal zones.
- Many marine animals find food in intertidal zones.

Sea stars are exposed at low tide.

for hours at a time. They can then be stranded in the hot sun later the same day. Crabs, snails, and barnacles are some of the most common animals in the intertidal ecosystem. They use their shells to protect themselves from drying out when the tide goes out. These thick coverings also protect against powerful waves when the ocean water returns.

Intertidal species can be sensitive to extreme changes in their environment. Too little salt can make it hard for these species to survive. Climate change can cause major temperature changes in ocean water. This can also be difficult for intertidal species.

Intertidal zones provide food for many animals. Sea birds, such as gulls, often feast on the tiny fish in the shallow waters. Sea stars are a favorite food of both seagulls and otters.

THINK ABOUT IT

It is easier for predators to find small animals in intertidal zones when the tide moves out. How might certain species use the sand and rocks on the shoreline to hide from bigger animals?

People and Animals Depend on Mangroves

Mangroves are hot tropical swamps. They are located along the coastlines in tropical and subtropical regions. Salt water fills mangrove ecosystems during high tide. When the tide is low, mangroves are made up mainly of mud and tangled tree roots. Many birds, shellfish, snakes, and crocodiles depend on mangroves for survival.

Most of the world's plant life could not survive in this harsh environment. Mangrove plants store freshwater, much like plants found in deserts. Their thick and waxy leaves help hold the moisture inside the plant even when the surroundings are dry.

The word *mangrove* is used to describe many tree and shrub species that live in mangrove ecosystems. This vegetation is unique. It has a high tolerance for salt water. Mangrove species can

Mangrove trees grow where the water meets the shore.

Estuarine crocodiles are found in the mangroves in northern Australia.

survive in water that is 100 times saltier than other plants can endure. They have special glands. These glands help mangrove trees release extra salt through their leaves.

The most diverse mangroves are in Southeast Asia. But many are facing huge threats due to shrimp farming. Farmers remove mangroves to build ponds where they can grow shrimp. People who make their livings from this industry are hurting mangrove ecosystems with overfishing and pollution. More than half of the mangroves in India, the Philippines, and Vietnam have been destroyed in the past century.

164

Average height, in feet (50 m), of some mangrove trees in Ecuador.

- Mangrove trees survive in an environment most other trees could not tolerate.
- They release excess salt through their leaves.
- Southeast Asia contains more mangrove forests than anywhere else in the world.
- Shrimp farming is placing mangrove ecosystems at great risk.

Salt Marshes Change with the Tides

Salt marshes are areas along a coastline where thick stands of marsh grasses grow. When the tide comes in, marsh waters rise. They lower when the tide moves back out. Marshes are made up of marsh grasses rooted in deep mud and peat. Peat is made of decaying plants. The plants help large amounts of bacteria grow. The bacteria break down the decaying plants even more. Animals, such as crabs and shrimp, live on the bottom of the marsh. They eat the bacteria and decaying plant matter.

In the United States, South Carolina has the most salt marshes.

There are salt marshes throughout the world. In the United States, they are

INVASIVE SPECIES

Invasive species can pose big threats to salt marshes. These plants and animals do not grow or live in these marshes naturally. People have brought them into the new marsh areas. Invasive species spread quickly. They threaten an ecosystem by using up resources, such as the food that native species need to survive.

Egrets are often found in salt marshes.

most common along the southeast Atlantic and Gulf Coasts.

Birds, such as egrets and herons, are common in South Carolina's marsh ecosystem. They often perch near tide pools as the tide moves out. The birds wait patiently until they see fish and other marine animals moving in the shallow water. Then the birds feed on these bottom-dwelling creatures.

In the past, humans have been a threat to marsh ecosystems. People built homes and businesses in marsh areas. They added extra soil to the marshes and removed water to make solid ground. People also hurt marsh ecosystems by using chemicals to kill mosquitoes. Today, there are both state and federal laws to protect marshes and prevent people from harming them. As a result, most salt marshes are healthy ecosystems.

344,500
Number of acres (139,414 ha) of marshland in South Carolina.

- The water in salt marshes rises and lowers with the tides.
- Salt marshes are found throughout the world.
- Birds living in salt marshes eat bottom-dwelling animals, such as crabs and shrimp.

Estuaries Are the Nurseries of the Sea

Estuaries are partially enclosed areas where rivers meet the sea. They are unique because of their brackish water. This is a mixture of freshwater from a river and salt water from the ocean. There are large populations of fish in estuaries.

Estuaries serve a very important role. They are animal breeding grounds. They provide many fish and

The view of an estuary near Skala Kallonis on Lésbos, Greece

River otters are common in Chesapeake Bay.

shellfish with an ideal place to lay their eggs. Two-thirds of the nation's commercial fish and seafood come from estuaries. Many birds use estuaries as nesting grounds. Even marine mammals, such as otters, depend on estuaries. They are safe places for mammals to give birth to their young.

Estuaries can include smaller ecosystems. Marshes and wetlands are parts of estuaries. The largest estuary in the United States is Chesapeake Bay. It is found off the coast of Maryland. This estuary includes marshes and wetlands.

It is just one of more than 100 estuaries in the country.

Another major estuary in the United States is Galveston Bay. It is a large estuary in the Gulf of Mexico. It affects life far from its own ecosystem. For example, fish and crabs migrate out of estuaries when they mature. Animals such as the bottlenose dolphin eat these organisms.

Coral Reefs Are Diverse Ecosystems

Coral reefs are rocklike ridges that form in warm ocean water. Coral are not actually rocks. They are animals with rocklike skeletons. They live together in large groups called colonies. Many other animals and plants make their homes on or near coral reefs.

The best-known coral reef is the Great Barrier Reef. It is off the coast of northeastern Australia. More than 3,000 smaller reefs make up this huge ecosystem. The Great Barrier Reef stretches more than 1,243 miles (2,000 km) along the coastline. It can be seen from outer space. This ecosystem is home to sharks, sea turtles, and more than 30 types of marine mammals, such as dolphins.

Many marine species live in a coral colony in Koh Tao, Thailand.

Sea fans are a type of soft coral.

Another well-known coral reef is found in the Florida Keys off the coast of the southern United States. Many animals, such as snapper fish and spiny lobsters, depend on this ecosystem. It gives them food, shelter, and a place to reproduce.

Many reefs around the world are suffering. One of the main reasons is bleaching. This is the loss of algae that live in coral. Algae give coral some of their nutrition. Rising water temperatures cause coral to lose their algae. They turn white. Bleached coral is more prone to disease. In 2016, the Great Barrier Reef lost one-third of its coral to bleaching. Pollution is also harming many coral ecosystems around the world.

1,500
Number of fish species in the Great Barrier Reef.

- Coral reef ecosystems are made up of animals with rocklike skeletons.
- Australia's Great Barrier Reef is so large it can be seen from space.
- Corals living on reefs around the world are struggling due to climate change and pollution.

Lagoons Come in Many Shapes and Sizes

Lagoons are shallow bodies of water that are separated from the rest of the ocean by landmasses. In some cases, long, narrow islands of sand sit between a lagoon and the open ocean. They are called barrier islands. Other natural structures can also separate lagoons from the rest of the sea. They include coral reefs or sandbars.

The warm waters of the Blue Lagoon in Iceland are a popular place for tourists.

39,537
Number of acres (16,000 ha) that make up the Lake Nokoué lagoon.

- Land masses, such as islands and sandbars, separate lagoons from the open ocean.
- Sea level has a major effect on the size and structure of a lagoon.
- The amount of freshwater and salt water varies from one lagoon to another.
- Some lagoons contain more freshwater or salt water at different times of the year.

Aitutaki is a lagoon in the Cook Islands.

The size and depth of lagoons can vary greatly. Lagoons are largest and deepest where the sea level is high. These lagoons look like lakes. Where the sea level is lowest, lagoons are similar to wetlands. Whether they are big or small, lagoons provide homes for many animals and plants.

HAPUA ECOSYSTEMS

Hapua ecosystems are lagoons near river mouths. The rivers create the lagoons by carving deep channels that run along the coastline. The lagoons are often filled with freshwater. Almost all hapua ecosystems are found in New Zealand. The strong ocean tides have a major effect on these lagoons. Over time, the pounding waves reshape the coastline.

Some lagoons with more land between them and the open sea have more freshwater than those with smaller barriers. The amount of salt in some lagoons even changes by the season. Lake Nokoué is a lagoon on the coast of Benin in western Africa. During the rainy season, this lagoon becomes an almost entirely freshwater area. It is more brackish during the dry season.

All fish need a certain amount of salt in their bodies. Fish that live in lagoons have adapted to both saltwater and freshwater environments. They use the small amounts of salt in fresh waters. Then they release excess amounts of salt when the water becomes brackish.

Oceans Are Filled with Fascinating Creatures

From reefs to marshes, marine ecosystems contain many life-forms. Marine animals come in all colors, shapes, and sizes. The bright blue and orange mandarinfish lives near Indonesia and Malaysia. It grows to just one to two inches (2.5 to 5.1 cm) long. Whale sharks are giants of the sea. Living in the tropics, some of them grow to 65 feet (20 m) long.

The sea is home to some of the most unusual animals on the planet. Jellyfish, sea horses, and squid are just a few of the unique species that live in the oceans. The box jellyfish

Mandarinfish come from the Pacific Ocean.

A SURPRISE ATTACK

Sea anemones look like underwater flowers. But these life-forms are actually animals. Anemones spend most of their lives attached to rocks or coral. Instead of hunting for food, they wait for prey, such as fish, to come to them. As soon as fish touch their tentacles, anemones sting them. This releases a paralyzing venom. Anemones then use their tentacles to move the fish to their mouths.

The box jellyfish is one of the most venomous marine animals.

has 24 eyes. Male sea horses give birth to babies called fry. Many types of squid can change the color and texture of their skin almost instantly. This helps them blend into their environments.

Some marine animals do not look like animals at all. Sponges look more like plants. But they are the simplest multicellular animals. They do not have nerves, muscles, or internal organs. Most sponges eat bacteria and other single-celled organisms.

500 million

Age, in years, of the oldest jellyfish fossils found on Earth.

- All marine ecosystems contain animals of many colors, shapes, and sizes.
- Some marine animals are among the most unusual creatures on the planet.
- Some animal species look more like plants than animals.

Marine Plants Provide Safe Havens for Animals

Plants play many roles in marine ecosystems. One of the most important is adding oxygen to the water. This helps create a healthy environment for the many animals within these ecosystems and beyond. Approximately 70 percent of the oxygen in Earth's atmosphere is produced by marine plants.

Plants provide food for many tiny marine creatures. Some animals, such as sea turtles, feast on sea grasses. These plants also offer shelter to small life-forms. They

Kelp is a type of plant that lives in shallow ocean waters and grows in underwater forests.

190

Distance, in feet (58 m), from the ocean surface to the deepest-growing sea grasses.

- Marine plants add oxygen to ocean water.
- Plants provide food and shelter for marine animals.
- Algae are among the most important plants in the oceans and on the planet.

Sea grasses face many dangers around the world.

help protect many animals so they can live long enough to reproduce. Without plants, many marine species would have nowhere to hide from predators.

Over the past century, nearly 30 percent of sea grass meadows have died. Bad storms with high winds are one reason for the decline. Pollution and damage from humans also cause problems. Anchors and boat propellers can cut into sea grasses and kill them.

When most people think of plants, they picture leafy green or flowering species. Certain types of marine plants do flower. But most do not look like plants we see on land. Some of the most common plants in the oceans are algae. These plants have no stems, roots, or leaves.

KEEPING THINGS STABLE

Sea grasses are types of marine plants that flower. Unlike algae, sea grasses have roots. These roots help keep sediment on the ocean floor in place. Sea grasses also slow water movement by absorbing ocean waves. This helps keep smaller marine animals from being swept away.

The Deep Sea Is a Mysterious Place

The deep sea is a vast ecosystem. It is the largest habitat on Earth. More than two-thirds of the planet is covered with water more than one mile (1.6 km) deep. The deepest point of the ocean is 6.8 miles (11 km) from the surface.

The deep sea is a cold and dark place. Most of the water is approximately 35 degrees Fahrenheit (1.7°C). But the temperature can dip as low as 28 degrees Fahrenheit (–2.2°C). Water normally starts to freeze by this point,

Anglerfish have adapted to live in the deep sea.

DO NOT DISTURB

Scientists often collect animals to study. But it is not easy to collect animals from the deep sea. Many deep-sea life-forms die on their way to the ocean's surface. This is due to changes in pressure and temperature as they rise up through the water. For this reason, marine biologists must observe deep-sea animals in their natural habitats.

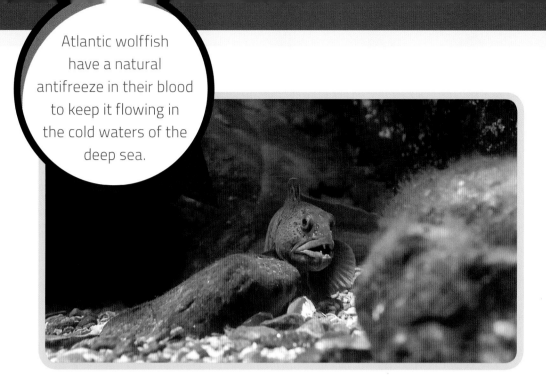

Atlantic wolffish have a natural antifreeze in their blood to keep it flowing in the cold waters of the deep sea.

but the ocean's salt lowers the freezing point of the water. Many deep-sea areas have never been lit by the sun. Still, life thrives in them. Instead of using the sun for energy, deep-sea animals eat bacteria or each other.

Some marine ecosystems have been affected by climate change. But deep-sea ecosystems have been thriving for billions of years. One of the main reasons is that people do not live in the deep sea. Scientists have recorded global warming in many parts of the world in recent years. But the water temperatures of the deep sea have remained steady since 2005.

17,000
Number of animal species known to live in the deep sea.

- Water more than one mile (1.6 km) deep covers more than two-thirds of the planet.
- Sunlight has never reached many areas of the deep sea.
- Many animals that live in the deep sea survive by eating bacteria.
- Deep-sea ecosystems have thrived for billions of years.

The Seafloor Is Mountainous in Places

The water near the coastlines of each continent is fairly shallow. Here, the ocean floor is called the continental shelf. It slopes deeper the farther it gets from the shoreline. In most places, the continental shelf is no more than 650 feet (198 m) from the water's surface. But in the deep sea, it can be as much as 55 times deeper. Scientists still have a lot to learn about the ocean floor of the deep sea.

Not all parts of the seafloor are flat. Just like dry land, the ocean's bottom includes many types of terrain. Mountains, plateaus, and trenches all lie deep beneath the ocean's surface. Some of the mountains are even larger than the Alps, one of the world's tallest mountain ranges.

Scientists use special equipment, such as diving bells, to study the ocean floor.

There are underwater volcanoes and earthquakes on some parts of the ocean floor. Underwater eruptions release chemicals that would be poisonous to most life above the ocean's surface. But they provide nutrients for deep-sea bacteria. The bacteria nourish life-forms that live on the ocean floor. Crustaceans use the bacteria as food, for example.

A wide variety of sponges and corals cling to the seafloor. Sea sponges and sea cucumbers live in the mud. Worms measuring eight feet (2.4 m) long grow around vents, or openings, in the earth.

The sea cucumber is one of the creatures that lives on the ocean floor.

HOT AND COLD

Vents and volcanoes on the seafloor create big temperature differences in small spaces. Some animals can live in water that is very hot and cold at the same time. Tube worms spend most of their lives with their upper bodies in water that is 37 degrees Fahrenheit (2.8°C). Their lower bodies are in water that is 392 degrees Fahrenheit (200°C).

5

Percentage of the ocean floor that has been mapped in detail.

- The ocean floor near the continents is called the continental shelf.
- The seafloor has mountains, plateaus, and trenches.
- Deep-sea volcanoes release chemicals that nourish bacteria in the water.

23

People Affect Most Marine Ecosystems

People can affect marine ecosystems in many ways. Some people live near the ocean. Others make a living fishing in marine waters. Even tourists who visit popular vacation spots, such as the Caribbean islands, can impact marine ecosystems.

People build homes and other structures near the ocean. This can hurt or kill many life-forms. Some resorts have removed mangrove forests and sea grasses to make beaches for tourists. Large numbers of tourists at certain beaches have disturbed nesting grounds for

Many people enjoy going to the beach, but it can be harmful to marine ecosystems.

500
Number of ocean areas where pollution has killed off most marine life.

- Some tourist resorts have destroyed mangrove forests and sea grasses.
- Large numbers of tourists make it difficult for many animal species to nest on beaches.
- Overfishing has reduced the populations of some marine species.
- Cruise ships leave pollution in marine ecosystems.

Cruise ships cause pollution in oceans.

animals such as sea turtles. In some places, people have even built piers right on top of coral reefs.

The ocean produces many types of fish and seafood. People who live in or visit coastal areas enjoy eating these foods. But tourism and growing demand for seafood have caused many places to become overfished. Some ocean animals simply cannot reproduce fast enough to keep up with the high demand.

People have caused a lot of pollution in marine ecosystems. Cruise ships leave a huge amount of waste in the world's oceans. Some ships dump garbage into the sea. Others release sewage from sinks and toilets into ocean water.

THINK ABOUT IT

Responsible fishing does not hurt marine ecosystems. Problems arise when people take too many of a certain species from the sea. Find one or two sentences in the main text that support this point.

People Can Help Care for Marine Ecosystems

Many humans have hurt marine ecosystems. But people can also make a positive difference for oceans and their many life-forms. The first step is learning to make the best choices. When you visit coastal regions, look for signs that mark protected areas, and stay away from them.

When you spend time at a beach or on the water in a boat, do not litter. You can even pick up trash that other people have left behind. Organizing a group cleanup at a beach can be both fun and good for the environment.

When eating at coastal restaurants, order only

Cleaning up a local beach is one way to help marine ecosystems.

Some people take coral from the ocean to make necklaces.

dishes made from sustainable fish and seafood. Also, think carefully before buying souvenirs. Items made from coral or tortoiseshell hurt marine animals.

You can also help marine ecosystems by supporting an organization that protects oceans and their many inhabitants. You might choose a group that is known worldwide. Greenpeace International, the Sierra Club, and the World Wildlife Fund are just a few well-known groups. You can also donate time or money to a smaller, local group that helps marine ecosystems.

40

Number of countries where the World Wildlife Fund works to improve marine ecosystems.

- People can make a positive difference in the health of the world's oceans.
- Both large and small environmental organizations help improve the condition of marine ecosystems.
- Doing research before eating out or buying products from the sea is important.

Marine Food Web

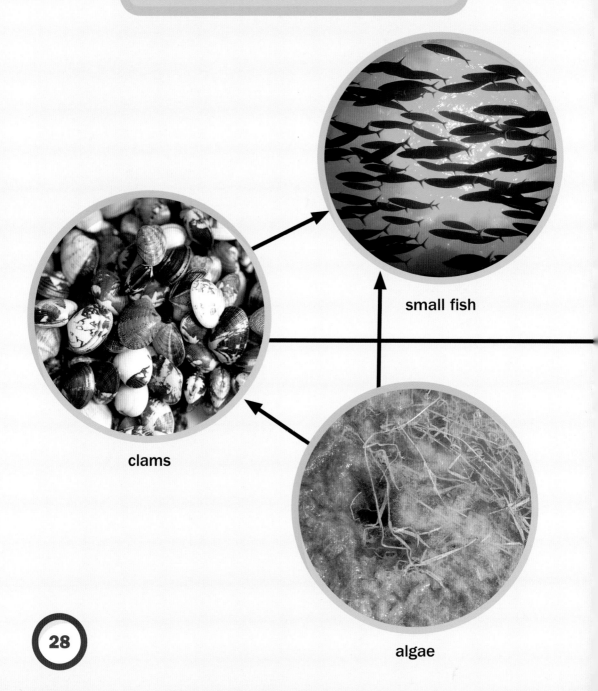

small fish

clams

algae

tiger shark

sea grasses

loggerhead turtle

box jellyfish

Glossary

adapted
Changed to fit a situation.

algae
A plantlike organism that grows in water.

bacteria
Single-celled organisms that break down dead tissues and recycle nutrients.

crustaceans
Animals with hard external shells that often live in the ocean, such as lobsters.

multicellular
An organism that has many cells.

native species
A species that naturally lives and grows in a certain place.

organisms
People, plants, animals, or microbes.

peat
A dark material that is left behind by decaying plants.

souvenirs
Items that serve as a reminder of a trip.

sustainable
Able to be maintained at a certain level.

tolerance
The ability to put up with something harmful or unpleasant.

For More Information

Books

Chambers, Catherine. *Stickmen's Guide to Oceans in Layers*. Minneapolis, MN: Hungry Tomato, 2016.

Gagne, Tammy. *Coral Reef Ecosystems*. Minneapolis, MN: ABDO Publishing, 2016.

Green, Jen. *Oceans in 30 Seconds*. Irvine, CA: Walter Foster, Jr., 2016.

Visit 12StoryLibrary.com

Scan the code or use your school's login at **12StoryLibrary.com** for recent updates about this topic and a full digital version of this book. Enjoy free access to:

- Digital ebook
- Breaking news updates
- Live content feeds
- Videos, interactive maps, and graphics
- Additional web resources

Note to educators: Visit 12StoryLibrary.com/register to sign up for free premium website access. Enjoy live content plus a full digital version of every 12-Story Library book you own for every student at your school.

Index

About the Author

Tammy Gagne has written more than 150 books for both adults and children. She resides in northern New England with her husband and son. One of her favorite pastimes is visiting schools to talk to children about the writing process.

READ MORE FROM 12-STORY LIBRARY

Every 12-Story Library book is available in many formats. For more information, visit 12StoryLibrary.com.